Les instincts de Giuseppe Verdi (1813–1901) pour trouver le bon matériel l'ont conduit à définir la compréhension de l'opéra par le grand public. Grâce à des œuvre telles *Aida* et *Rigoletto*, rares sont les personnes qui n'ont jamais entendu son travail. Sur ce carnet figure un extrait de sa correspondance. Que ses instincts naturels et puissants vivent à jamais sur les grandes scènes et que son héritage inspire votre propre main.

Mit seiner Intuition für die richtigen Inhalte schaffte Giuseppe Verdi (*1813, †1901) Werke, die das allgemeine Verständnis von Oper prägen. Dank Meisterwerken wie *Aida* und *Rigoletto* gibt es unter uns nur wenige, die nie der Musik von Verdi gelauscht haben. Hier ist ein Auszug aus Verdis Korrespondenz abgebildet. Möge seine natürliche, raffinierte Intuition auf den Bühnen der Welt ewig weiterleben und sein Vermächtnis Ihre Hand führen.

Grazie al suo istinto Verdi (1813-1901) creò composizioni che definiscono la comprensione dell'opera da parte del pubblico generale, e per merito di capolavori come *Aida* e *Rigoletto* sono pochi coloro che non hanno mai ascoltato un'opera di Verdi. Il frammento della missiva di Verdi riprodotto sulla nostra copertina vuole essere un invito a lasciarti ispirare dal naturale e raffinato istinto di questo compositore grande compositore.

El instinto de Giuseppe Verdi (1813-1901) para hallar el material adecuado lo llevó a crear obras que acercaron la ópera al gran público. Gracias a obras maestras como *Aida* y *Rigoletto*, son pocos los que nunca han escuchado algo de su música. Aquí reproducimos un extracto de la correspondencia de Verdi. Ojalá su sagacidad y su instinto natural pervivan por siempre en los grandes escenarios y su legado le inspire a la hora de escribir.

ジュゼッペ・ヴェルディ(1813–1901年)は適切な素材を選びとるという、持って生まれた才能によって、大衆のオペラの理解を決定づけたといっても過言ではない数々の作品を作り上げました。『アイーダ』や『リゴレット』といった有名な名作により、誰もが1度はヴェルディの作品を耳にしたことがあるのではないでしょうか。本装丁では、ヴェルディの手紙から抜粋した直筆の文章をデザインに用いています。ヴェルディの生まれながらの才能が舞台の上で永遠に生き続け、そのレガシーが皆さんの創作のきっかけとなることを願ってやみません。

paperblanks®

EMBELLISHED MANUSCRIPTS

Verdi, Carteggio

Giuseppe Verdi's (1813–1901) instincts for finding the right material led him to create works that virtually define the general public's understanding of opera. Thanks to masterworks such as *Aida* and *Rigoletto*, few are those who have never heard Verdi's work. Featured here is an excerpt from Verdi's correspondence. May his natural and canny instincts live forever on the great stages and his legacy inspire your own hand.

ISBN: 978-1-4397-2915-1
MINI FORMAT   176 PAGES   LINED
DESIGNED IN CANADA